Bullets

BY THE BILLION

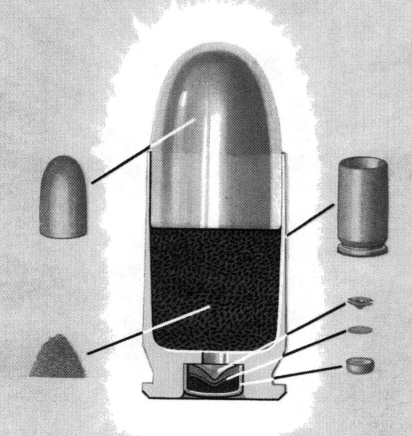

Cross-section of .45 caliber cartridge.

Bullets

BY THE BILLION

by Wesley W. Stout

Chrysler Corporation
Detroit, Michigan 1946

Foreword

THIS *is the story of the only Chrysler Corporation plant where billions of any finished product were made during the war. It is the story of our assembly plant in Evansville, Indiana which made ammunition in astronomical amounts.*

Before the war Plymouth passenger cars and Dodge trucks were assembled here by 650 people. By September, 1943 the working force had increased to twenty times that number and extensive additions had been made to the plant's facilities. Most of the management and supervision were loaned from Detroit, but the largest part of the working force was drawn from homes, offices, farms and little stores and shops in an area seventy-five miles around the city.

These people did eight important war jobs. They

made more than three billion .45 caliber cartridges; almost a half a billion .30 caliber cartridges; hundreds of thousands of rounds of other special types of ammunition; specially packed a billion and a half rounds of ammunition for use in the Pacific; reconditioned 1662 General Sherman tanks; rebuilt 4,000 Army trucks; delivered 800,000 tank grousers and when the war ended, had just got under way on an order for 7,000,000 firebombs.

Each of these jobs was performed for the United States Army Ordnance Department, except the firebomb which came under the jurisdiction of the Chemical Warfare Service. Production was greatly assisted by the enthusiastic support and effort of these two organizations and by the aid and cooperation of the people of Evansville. The achievement of this Plant is another example of how peacetime developed engineered production methods were put to the service of the United States in time of war.

K. T. KELLER,
President

Aerial view of the explosives and loading area, half a mile from the factory and connected by a specially designed conveyor.

The Chrysler Evansville arsenal, new office building in foreground. In 1941 it had been an assembly plant turning out 275 Plymouths daily.

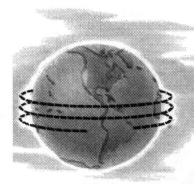

If all the cartridges made in the Evansville Plant were laid end to end, they would reach 2.8 times around the world.

How many is a billion?

A few days after Pearl Harbor, K. T. Keller was in Washington headquarters of OPM. As he was leaving, he was asked if Chrysler had an available factory with a lot of water.

"We have a Plymouth assembly plant at Evansville, Indiana, on the Ohio river," said Mr. Keller.

"How big is it?"

"Four to five hundred thousand square feet."

"Come with me," said the OPM man and led him to the then lieutenant colonel, now General Guy H. Drewry of Army Ordnance.

The Army, Drewry said, needed three to five billions of .45 caliber cartridges; could Chrysler make these at Evansville?

"Yes," said Keller.

The Ordnance officer was startled. "Do you always make up your mind this fast?" he asked.

"Not always, Colonel, but we have been hearing more and more about billions in recent years," Chrysler's president explained. "I still can't imagine

1

C. L. Jacobson, General Manager, Chrysler Evansville Plant.

what a billion is like, so I'd like to make billions of something and find out."

This is how Chrysler came to make more than three billions of cartridges between late June of 1942 and April 20, 1944, in this Evansville plant where, in 1941, a force of 650 men had been assembling 275 Plymouth cars daily. The total was 3,264,281,914, including 96% of all .45 caliber ammunition made for the armed forces. Another billion and a half rounds were repacked for Ordnance. Employment reached 12,650 at the peak, twenty times the plant's peacetime normal.

This was done by an organization in which there were not five men of the meagerest previous experi-

B. M. Bickford,
Factory Manager.

R. Christman,
Chief Engineer.

R. P. Jones,
Superintendent
Explosives Area.

ence in ammunition or explosives. It was done in spite of the cartridge cases having been changed from brass to steel, unprecedented in small arms, just as Evansville was testing its first brass cartridges; in spite of other radical changes in the kind and amounts of cartridges asked of the converted automobile assembly plant.

Chrysler began at Evansville by making something it never had made before. With the change to steel cases, it undertook to make something new to the small arms art. In fewer than six months it was turning out millions of rounds daily of steel-cased cartridges accepted by the Army for combat use in all areas.

I. Boldt, Fac-
ry Superintendent.

H. V. Holland,
Assistant to
General Manager.

Robert Dickman,
Assistant
Plant Engineer.

Three billions plus is a meaningless sum until you try to count it. Suppose that you could tally a hundred bullets a minute: working eight hours a day, six days a week and fifty-two weeks a year, you would be 218 years in reaching 3,264,281,914, or from five years before George Washington was born down to this moment. Or if you prefer end-to-end statistics, Evansville cartridges, averaging a little more than an inch long, would have reached 2.8 times around the earth at its broadest.

Three billions is no staggering manufacturing quantity in itself, of course. Making that many pins, bolts or other simple piece stamped out in one or two operations in endless repetition is a commonplace of

4

industry. A gun is a precision mechanism, however, and these cartridges had seven parts and passed through 48 processing operations. They had to be so exact as to survive 334 distinct inspections, including the firing of more than a million rounds monthly on the plant's test ranges.

On a cost and fee contract, the Corporation manufactured this ammunition at well below its cost estimate.

FROM CARTRIDGES TO TANKS

In World War I the Government had set up sixteen companies of no previous experience in small arms ammunition, none of which produced a cartridge fired in that war. In this war, Chrysler, United States Rubber and Kelly-Springfield Tire were the newcomers in this field. Wholly inexperienced, Evansville soon was making more .45 cartridges every day than all American sources combined had made in a year in peace; and shortly it added a line of .30 caliber carbine shells.

Of 1,033 lots of .45 caliber ammunition, all were accepted by Ordnance. One of 277 lots of .30 carbine cartridges was found slightly high in pressure, was rejected and torn down. Total rejections, therefore, were well less than .1% of production.

With an ample supply of small calibers, Ordnance closed down most small arms plants in the spring of 1944. The Evansville plant shifted from cartridges

Three of the principal weapons using Evansville-built cartridges. From left to right, a .30 caliber carbine, a .45 caliber submachine gun and a .45 caliber automatic pistol.

weighing seven-tenths of an ounce, about that of a cigar, to the rebuilding of 35-ton tanks, then to rebuilding Army trucks and to making 800,000 grousers for tank tracks—literally tank overshoes for better traction in mud—and, finally, just before the war ended, to large incendiary bombs.

EVANSVILLE ORIGINALLY A DODGE PLANT

The Evansville property came to Chrysler through Dodge Brothers who had got it in turn from Graham Brothers who had made motor trucks there before World War I. Many of the country's early school buses had been made there by Dodge. Chrysler carried on truck making there from 1928 until 1932. The plant then was idle until 1935 when the Corporation began to assemble Plymouths and half-ton trucks in it. Many of these were shipped by river barge up the Tennessee to Guntersville, Alabama, or down the Mississippi and through the inter-coastal canal to Texas for redistribution.

This operation was one of the first to be pinched off by the war. Two other large industries of the town also were closed by priorities. Evansville was left a distressed area by the end of 1941. The mayor, the unions, the Chamber of Commerce and the Indiana Congressional delegation were besieging the Corporation to restore the Chrysler payroll, while the Corpo-

Cartridge cups entering the normalizing furnaces where, by means of heat, the strains set up in the blanking were healed.

ration in turn was doing its best to find war work suitable to this plant. No one foresaw that the war soon was to expand the city from 97,000 to 150,000 and make it one of the most crowded centers in America.

When Mr. Keller returned from Washington, he sent for Charles L. Jacobson, Vice President in charge of sales for the Chrysler division.

"Colonel Drewry* in Washington has been talking to us about making cartridges at Evansville," Mr. Keller told him. "A first step is to see the district Ordnance people at Cincinnati and get their approval of the plant. If we can get such a contract, it will be

*Now General Drewry

8

The cartridge case began as a cup, blanked from a sheet of metal; it then was formed into a case in two draws.

useful to the Army and keep the Evansville working force employed."

Charley Jacobson was in Cincinnati the next morning, a Saturday, and persuaded the Ordnance office to have a survey officer in Evansville on Monday morning to report on the plant's suitability for the job. On Sunday, Jacobson saw the plant for the first time and put together a little illustrated prospectus to carry to Washington.

He reported back to Detroit on Tuesday, was in Washington Wednesday showing his booklet to OPM and to Ordnance. There was not enough brass for existing cartridge contracts, the shortage one of rolling mills rather than of copper, and Ordnance was creating no new cartridge facilities until it could see where the brass was coming from. But with an estimated deficit of two and a half billions of .45 caliber rounds, an exception was to be made in this caliber.

On Friday, Jacobson carried back to Detroit a letter of intent for the making of 5,000,000 .45 caliber cartridges daily. The first intention was to combine the Evansville Chrysler and Briggs plants for the

Reels of lead wire fed into automatic machines which formed the bullet slugs; belts carried the slugs away to inspection.

ammunition contract, the latter supplying Plymouth bodies in peacetimes, but Briggs now was committed to the Navy for aircraft parts. All could be done, it then was decided, on the Chrysler property except for the addition of some powder magazines and a primer manufacturing and loading area, separated from the assembly plant. The primer is the detonator of a cartridge, loaded with a minute amount of high explosive.

Jacobson was at Frankford Arsenal in Philadelphia studying the set-up of that permanent Army gun and shell factory when Colonel Schaeffer phoned him

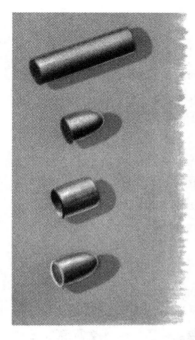

jumping the order 7,500,000 rounds daily. The following day, Ordnance phoned that it wanted 10,000,000 daily, one quarter of these to be tracer bullets.

These sudden increases in the order were said to have been a precaution against a possible invasion of the East or West coasts. The War Department was reported to be planning to issue side arms and submachine guns to hastily mustered civilian auxiliaries.

Then, before January was out, Colonel Schaeffer was phoning again that Ordnance must have 12,500,000 daily, one fourth tracer bullets. Jacobson doubted that the labor and facilities would exist for an order two and a half times the first proposal. Evansville already was on the boom. The news was just out that the Navy was coming to build landing craft in a big way.

Woman inspector checking the dimensions of a bullet slug.

Servel, Hoosier Lamp and Briggs had war contracts and Republic Aircraft was about to build a large new plant to make the P-47 "Thunderbolt" plane.

He took his problem to Detroit. "Charley, in war you can't say no," Mr. Keller told him. "If they want 12,500,000 rounds a day, we'll have to give it to them somehow. Can't we tie in with some other Evansville factory?"

These machines made the first draw of the cartridge case. Standard for brass, all equipment had to be adjusted for steel.

A battery of trimming machines. The cartridge case had to be trimmed after each draw.

Jacobson returned to Indiana and talked with the Sunbeam refrigerator people who were making shell fuses but had unused capacity and were interested in any other war job for which their facilities and personnel might be suited.

The Sunbeam Company was particularly qualified to assist Chrysler because it had tool makers which Chrysler Corporation needed at the time and because it had floor space which could be used to produce some cartridge cases.

The result was that Sunbeam and Chrysler signed a contract whereby the refrigerator plant agreed to make the perishable tools needed for the ammunition

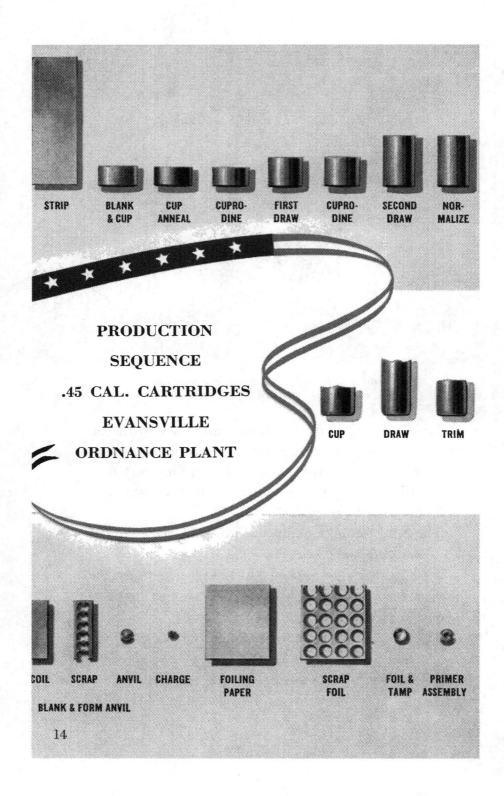

STRIP | BLANK & CUP | CUP ANNEAL | CUPRO-DINE | FIRST DRAW | CUPRO-DINE | SECOND DRAW | NOR-MALIZE

PRODUCTION

SEQUENCE

.45 CAL. CARTRIDGES

EVANSVILLE

ORDNANCE PLANT

CUP | DRAW | TRIM

COIL | SCRAP | ANVIL | CHARGE | FOILING PAPER | SCRAP FOIL | FOIL & TAMP | PRIMER ASSEMBLY

BLANK & FORM ANVIL

14

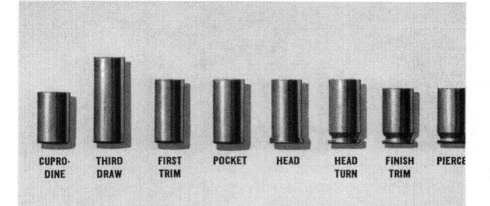

| CUPRO-DINE | THIRD DRAW | FIRST TRIM | POCKET | HEAD | HEAD TURN | FINISH TRIM | PIERCE |

| LEADWIRE | SLUG | JACKET | SLUG | BULLET | COIL | SCRAP | CUP |

BLANK & CUP

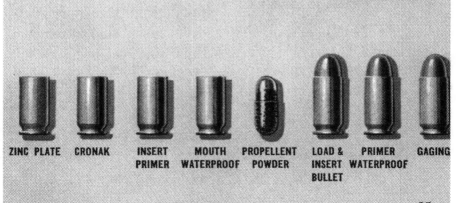

| ZINC PLATE | CRONAK | INSERT PRIMER | MOUTH WATERPROOF | PROPELLENT POWDER | LOAD & INSERT BULLET | PRIMER WATERPROOF | GAGING |

job and 40% of the cartridge cases, which Chrysler Corporation would later load, pack and ship.

The formal contract with the Government was signed on Washington's Birthday, 1942, the plant capacity rated at 12,500,000 daily on a 3-shift, 24-hour operation. This done, Mr. Keller asked Charley Jacobson how he would like to manage the arsenal.

The dismantling of the former Plymouth assembly lines began next day. Five days later, 92 future supervisors, the first of many such groups, left for Frankford Arsenal for training on such machines as they would oversee later. Toward the end of March, grading began on the explosives area and the contract was let for tripling the administration building to house the necessary staff.

Jacobson's immediate job was to build an organization. When he went to Fred Zeder of Chrysler Engineering seeking an engineer, Zeder suggested that Bob Christman was the

Inspector checking weight of a bullet slug on sensitive torsion balancer scales.

First visual inspection of .45 caliber cases after the first trim. Women sorted out defective cases and bits of trim which had escaped the separators.

one man around with special knowledge of firearms. Christman, since dead, was reared in the Ten Sleep country of Wyoming. At fourteen, his father had given him a pair of .45 Colt Frontier revolvers and taught him how to use them, setting the boy off on a lifetime hobby. Christman became chief engineer.

Ralph Jones of the Engineering division had come to Chrysler as paint and lacquer expert. Lacquers, like propellant powders, are mostly nitrocellulose. Jones became superintendent of the explosives area. B. M.

Cartridge cases emerging from hydrogen embrittlement relief ovens, a form of heat treatment after zinc plating.

Final trimming operation in the forming of the .45 caliber case of the cartridge fired in the .45 automatic pistol and many machine guns.

Bickford, who had managed the assembly plant before the war, remained as factory manager. F. W. Boldt, factory superintendent, was one of a very few with previous experience in ammunition; he had come from the St. Louis Arsenal where he had had one year's experience with cartridges.

In mid-May Ordnance cancelled the tracer bullets as no longer needed, transferring this 25% of quota to .45 ball cartridges. One hundred acres East of the assembly plant had been condemned by the Government and a dairy and 28 homes moved off this land.

These machines clad the soft lead bullet slug
with a copper jacket for greater accuracy of fire.

On it now, 120 special purpose tracer buildings were going up, this touchy stuff requiring a special cell for each loading operation. Cancellation made it possible to move all loading operations out of the main plant into some of these buildings, separating manufacturing from explosives by half a mile of open space.

Late on the night of June 30, 1942, ninety days from the breaking of ground for the expanded plant, Chrysler gunners began to test fire the first rounds of .45 caliber brass ball cartridges made from production

20

machines and tools. (Sample lots had been made by hand methods before this.) Steel sheets were rigged in the power house coal pile and the gunners fired from temporary shanties, the Ballistics building existing only on paper as yet. The cartridges fired, and accurately.

When the Evansville force came to work the next morning, they found an order from Washington to shift from brass to steel cases because of the acute shortage of brass. The order read: "to be made from the same machine tools as now installed in the plant," though all equipment was designed for brass.

A first necessity of a cartridge case is that it not corrode easily. Brass' resistance to corrosion is one of its virtues, steel's lack of resistance one of its weaknesses. A cartridge case must be elastic enough to

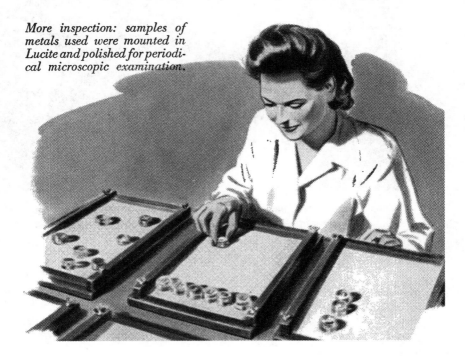

More inspection: samples of metals used were mounted in Lucite and polished for periodical microscopic examination.

Concentration on an inspection line: These eyes were charged with weeding out ten different defects in the cartridge case.

expand under the explosive charge, making a tight seal against the breech wall of the gun barrel, and yet spring back instantly for easy ejection of the case lest it jam the gun. Brass being three times springier than steel, it would be necessary to have a much higher yield strength in cartridge case steel, yet if steel is too hard it will split or crack.

The Corporation had set up in Evansville a very complete engineering laboratory of which it now had urgent need. There are as many different kinds of steel, not including alloys, as there are of wood, with as many varying qualities. The right kind of steel for cartridge cases had to be discovered by laboratory research, and always remembering the limitations of the production machinery on hand and on order, designed for brass.

SPECIAL STEEL REQUIRED

By means of microscopic photography and other metallurgical tests, Christman and his men came to the conclusion that they needed a certain steel technically described as "spheroidized, aluminum-cleaned, with a .13 to .18 carbon content."

The trouble was that no mill ever had made such a steel in quantity, the use of aluminum for purifying steel now was forbidden by WPB, and Christman's narrow range of 5/100ths of carbon content was much closer than anything to which steel mills were used. Chrysler got authority from WPB for the use of aluminum after Ordnance had approved the request, but the head metallurgist of the steel mill hesitated to approve the order until Chrysler men had made a special trip to Pittsburgh and met with the mill's production heads.

"What will happen if we make a batch of steel a point or two above or below your tolerances?" the head metallurgist wanted to know.

Christman got out his micro-photographs of the structure of the steel he sought. "We have satisfied ourselves," he explained, "that anything inside this .13 to .18 range will make good cases. We haven't the

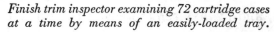

Finish trim inspector examining 72 cartridge cases at a time by means of an easily-loaded tray.

This machine water-proofed the neck of the case before insertion of the foiling patch and powder charge.

experience yet to say whether steels a little above or below this range also will make good cases, but if we find that they will, we'll be happy to take the steel."

"If that's the way it is, we'll do our part," agreed the steel men.

Steel forced a revolution in Evansville's tooling, for the tools which work on brass are not necessarily adapted to steel. Production tested out experimental tooling until it found a set-up which worked on steel. It is a long way, however, from the tool room where you can correct your errors by hand to the automatic

precision necessary to manufacturing millions of an item daily.

In the midst of the steel struggle, Washington cut small arms ammunition production by one third. If there had been a danger of invasion, it had passed, and supply was overtaking immediate needs. It first was planned to cancel undelivered machinery and tear down excess buildings in the explosives area. The machinery was far enough along, a check showed, that the cancellation cost would be 80% of the delivered cost.

The arsenal could have made 12,500,000 cartridges a day only by working around the clock. Chrysler recommended that the facilities be completed as planned and the plant stepped down to two 8-hour shifts. This would lower production by the same

In the explosives area: machines at right inserted high-explosive into primer cup and sealed it with foiling paper; machines at left assembled the anvil into primer cup.

one-third and save in six months, by avoiding the penalties of a third shift, as much as could be gained by cancellations. The fact that most explosions in small arms plants had occurred during the third or graveyard shift was an additional argument. Ordnance approved.

The first twenty experimental steel cartridges, drawn from a makeshift steel and made by hand, were test-fired July 7th, within two weeks of the change order. Production quantities of the proper steel could not be had before October, but a small lot was found in late July. Cartridges made from this batch satisfied Engineering that it had found the formula.

So, on Columbus Day, 1942, Evansville began to make production steel cases, with 140,000 run through

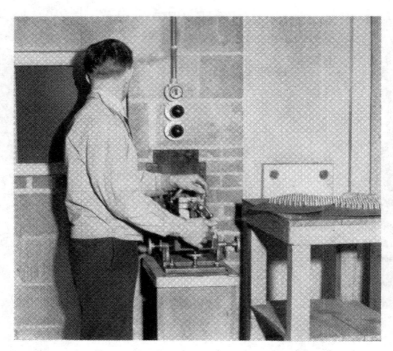

Firing fixed-rest guns at an enclosed target 50 feet away for accuracy testing.

the draw presses in two shifts. At the end of an Aberdeen Proving Grounds test that same October week, the Chrysler men were told to go back to Indiana and open the flood gates on .45 steel ammunition production.

The flood gates were not opened that easily. By November first, 500,000 rounds had been accepted by Ordnance and case casualties were running from zero to .05%, far under permissible limits. But the million rounds daily schedule set the arsenal for November was out of the question for lack of bright-annealing and normalizing furnaces adapted to steel. The ten furnaces installed for brass had to be rebuilt by their maker for steel and the first attempt to convert them was a failure.

Evansville was working on the corrosion problem at the same time. Some kind of plating of the steel case was imperative. Ordnance preferred zinc plating with Kronak, but asked Chrysler to canvass all possibilities. In time a double Kronak dipped case was adopted which gave a resistance nearly equal to that of brass.

Ordnance was shipping Evansville's steel cartridges to the service boards of the various using arms by November, and in December favorable reports began to come back. Among 650,000 rounds, the using arms had found a minimum of defects. The largest number of split cases in any lot was one seventh of the allowable percentage.

Then on January 16, 1943, came a letter from Ordnance stating that steel cartridges as made at

With this specially designed apparatus, a girl could be taught in a few minutes to check target sheets for velocity.

Evansville under the process developed by Chrysler in collaboration with Frankford Arsenal were authorized for combat use in all areas.

"Make all you can," Washington told the Corporation. With furnaces and plating equipment now in, steel cartridge production reached 103,000,000 rounds in January and was going strong in February.

WHEN A PISTOL IS NO HELP

In the midst of this, Evansville had been given a new job and a big one—to make .30 caliber carbine ammunition. An exploding carbine cartridge exerts 40,000 pounds to the square inch against 16,000 pounds in the .45 caliber, hence its non-corrosive primer is much "hotter" than that of the .45 and it uses nearly twice as much propellant powder. That powder is double-based, compounded of nitrocellulose and nitroglycerine. For easier extraction, the case carries a faint external taper from the mouth back about three fourths of its length, yet the inner wall must not reflect this taper, a tricky tooling and metallurgical problem. The arsenal began .30 carbine cartridge production in brass, but was given a development contract to convert to steel by May of 1943.

The .45 caliber pistol was the historic side-arm of the American Army, but it was purely a defensive weapon, its effective range about 50 yards. In modern warfare the number of support troops and rear ele-

Test-firing the .45 cartridge from an automatic pistol. Men who loved guns did this, marvelling that anyone could be found to pay them for shooting.

*Target sheets, after ten shots, came back to these
inspectors for the checking of accuracy of fire.*

ments has increased steadily. At the same time, the fluid tactics introduced by armored shock forces, airborne troops and paratroopers left artillery positions, communications centers, supply depots and the headquarters of the higher echelons so many sitting ducks against a rifle-bearing enemy, even though the infantry line in the immediate front may not have been broken.

To defend themselves, they needed an automatic or semi-automatic, hard-hitting weapon firing accurately up to 300 yards, and so light and mobile that carrying it would not get in the way of their normal duties. The existing carbine did not fill this bill.

Following the French collapse of May, 1940, Ordnance launched a contest for a new carbine, and eight designs had been entered by the following May. All failed in the tests which went on through the summer of 1941 until, at the last moment, Winchester entered the competition as an added starter with a semi-automatic carbine designed and made in six weeks. It

Chrysler set up an elaborate engineering laboratory at Evansville, and soon had urgent need of it.

won the prize hands down and became the M-1.

In the Fall as Ordnance began to speed up the M-1 program, it became evident that as .30 carbine production rose, that of .45 caliber cartridges must fall, for the carbine was to replace the pistol in most uses. When Chrysler was asked by Ordnance if it would consider converting some of its .45 capacity to carbine production, the Corporation was ready to make the changeover.

Ordnance pointed out grave difficulties, however. A principal one was the non-corrosive primer demanded by the using arms. The very small porthole which accentuates the gas mechanism of the M-1 is nearly impossible to keep clean in combat if a corrosive primer is used, it fouling the port quickly. The non-

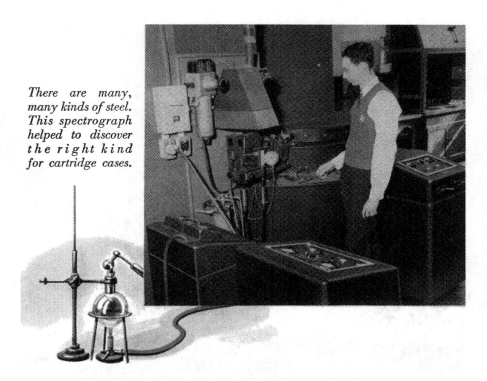

There are many, many kinds of steel. This spectrograph helped to discover the right kind for cartridge cases.

corrosive primer was a German creation and touchy stuff. If Chrysler tried to make it, it might be two years in getting the raw materials and learning its tricks. It would be simpler to buy it, if it could be bought—it was not to be had merely by asking for it.

There were two formulas, one owned by Remington, the other by Western Cartridge. Chrysler first studied the Remington process at Lake City, Mo., but much stainless steel pipe was necessary to it, and stainless was as scarce as sharks in the Ohio river. Too, lead styphnate, the base used by Remington, still is explosive in water and there were no facilities at Evansville for the safe disposal of waste.

Western Cartridge used a base desensitized by

35

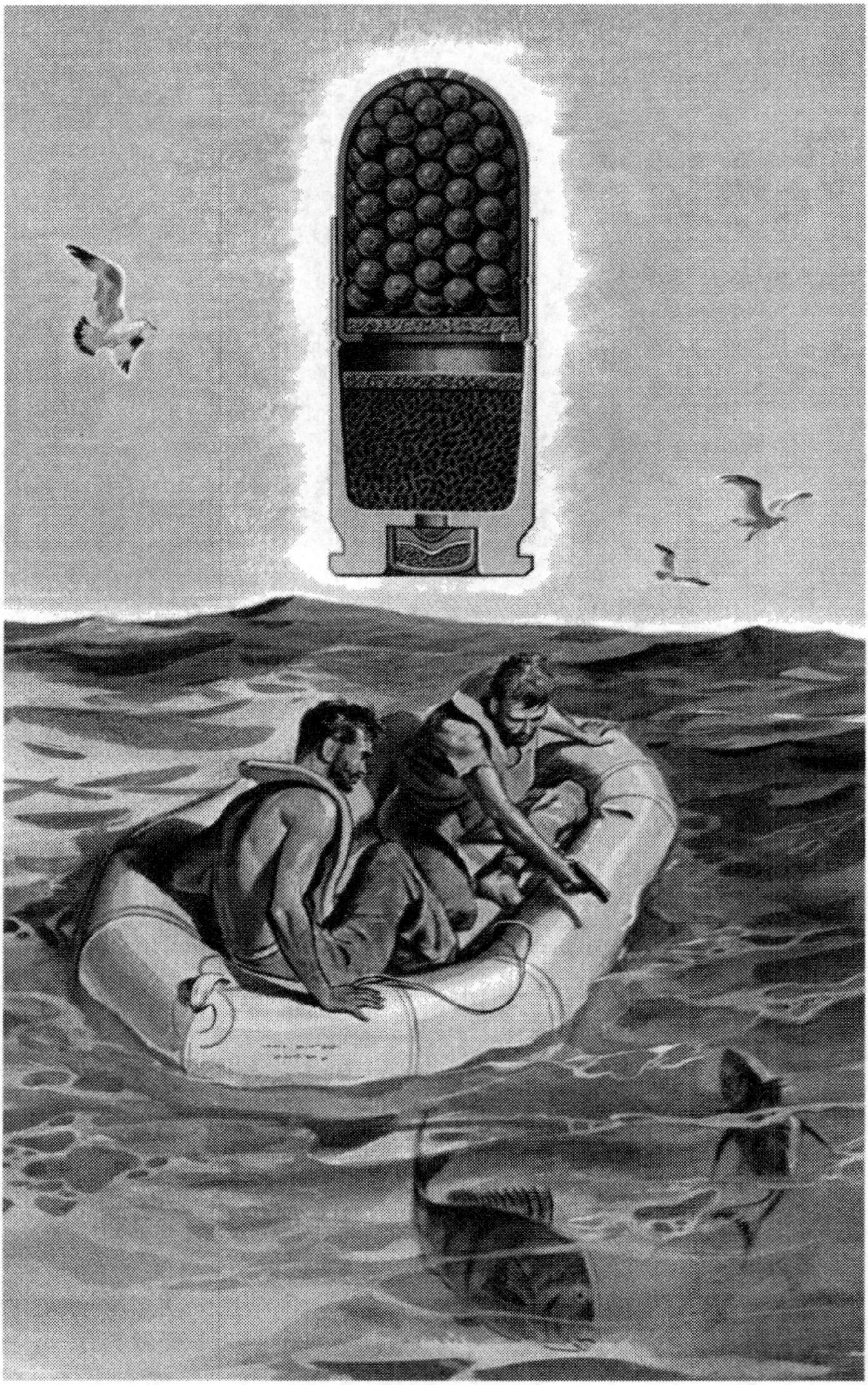

water. Evansville could store it under water in heated, barricaded buildings, getting rid of the wastes in its existing scrap furnaces. None of the other ingredients offered unusual difficulties, if Western would supply them, and Evansville's existing primer mixing machinery could be used.

John Olin, Western's founder and president, met with Mr. Keller and patriotically granted the Chrysler Corporation a patent agreement for the duration, lending Evansville a group of experts for a time and supplying the arsenal with the three prime ingredients.

The carbine contract was signed February 27, 1943, though long before this Evansville was converting part of its machinery. At the Advisory Board meeting in Chicago on February 18th it had been revealed

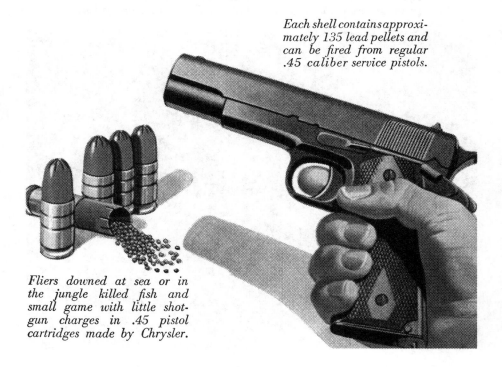

Each shell contains approximately 135 lead pellets and can be fired from regular .45 caliber service pistols.

Fliers downed at sea or in the jungle killed fish and small game with little shotgun charges in .45 pistol cartridges made by Chrysler.

that the supplementary contract for .30 carbine cartridges in steel was meeting with resistance among the using arms, where many were unconvinced that steel could be a satisfactory substitute for brass.

When Mr. Jacobson reported this to Mr. Keller, the latter said: "I do not know at this time what to say to you other than that we should do everything Ordnance wishes us to do short of meddling in what is purely a military decision. Ordnance knows how many and what calibers and kinds of bullets the Army needs and the amounts of metals available for making them. If they ask us to make steel cases, we should do the best job possible; if they want us to make brass cases, we'll make brass cases. The using

After 334 separate inspections by Chrysler watchers, the finished cartridges were placed in tote boxes for Government inspection.

Steel cases were bathed against corrosion in a dichromate solution by a machine which sorted and arranged them magnetically.

arms know what they want; Ordnance knows what it can supply, while we know nothing of these problems and should not try to influence their professional judgment."

A month earlier, Chrysler's president had written Mr. Jacobson: "I learned yesterday that future .45 caliber production is to be cut about a billion rounds, while future .30 carbine cartridge production is going up by about the same amount. While I understand that we have an order for the development of steel cases in the carbine ammunition, don't be surprised if you are asked to make brass while you are develop-

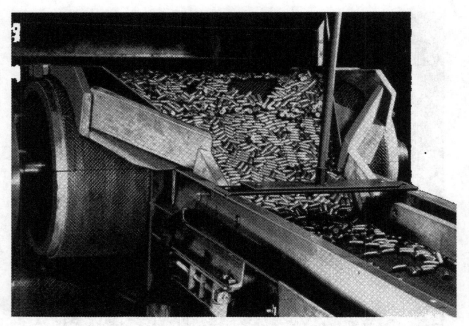

Cases emerging from an anti-corrosion bath at the rate of 103,200 an hour. They passed through a demagnetizer before reaching the belt.

ing steel. If we are going to get into the manufacture of the .30, it might be well to get started on brass and thereby have a good basis of comparison with the same product in steel."

Though he called the turn in part, Mr. Keller could not foresee all that was coming on the carbine cartridge. Ordnance would have preferred in 1941 to have tailored a new cartridge to the new gun, but seeking quick availability of manufacture in that critical year, it had adapted an existing self-loading cartridge to the new carbine. And though fundamentally an excellent weapon, there had not been time to sweat all the bugs out of it.

Engineering quickly whipped the metallurgical problems of the longer, tapered case, yet the cartridges would not function uniformly. They failed to feed, extract or eject surely. An Aberdeen Proving Grounds test of steel and brass cases fired alternately showed a trifling superiority for steel, but too many failures for both.

Baffled by variations they could not account for, Ordnance had an ultra high-speed motion picture made of the carbine in action. At 8,000 exposures a minute, the film was so deliberate that minutes seemed to pass while the hammer fell. This disclosed hitherto hidden minor flaws in the gun.

Cartridges were packed 50 to a carton at the rate of 540,000 an hour; then cartons were packed for shipment in heavy wooden boxes.

New production was corrected quickly and the carbines already issued to troops were repaired in the field, but Ordnance grew reluctant to push .30 steel cases against the prejudices of the soldier. Men who live or die by their weapons are conservative-minded about them. Steel cases were new. If a carbine jammed, the human inclination was to blame the new and strange factor. With brass again to be had, it would be easier to go on making brass cases than to convince the soldier that steel was as good.

NO COMPLAINTS AGAINST STEEL

The steel case of the .45 caliber was another matter. Here there had been no trouble with the weapons and so no suspicion lay against the cartridge in the minds of soldiers. Brig. Gen. James Kirk, chief of the Small Arms section, told Jacobson in November that he could find no complaints from the using arms against .45 steel. A few days later General Kirk wrote Mr. Keller:

"Since the Evansville plant has been so successful in developing a steel cartridge case meeting all the exacting military requirements, it is intended to continue this excellent cartridge in production in spite of the recent easing up of brass supply. As it can be seen at this moment, the only reason for a change in this policy would be adverse reports from the fighting front, which we have not had."

Completed cartridge packs moving by belt to the shipping dock. There were nearly six miles of motorized belt and gravity roller conveyors in the plant.

Another threat, however, loomed over the small arms industry. Up to the invasion of France, the Army used only a little of the ammunition stored up. With the surplus becoming unwieldly, Ordnance began to cut production schedules and in the late winter of 1943-44 it ordered a general shutdown of small arms plants. When we broke through the German lines in France later in 1944, cartridge consumption leaped so sharply that a number of these plants were reopened, but no shortage developed in either the .45 or .30 caliber carbine and Evansville, in any case, had been converted before then to rebuilding tanks.

Before the arsenal wound up its ammunition run,

it did two special jobs for Ordnance. In November, 1943, the Philadelphia Ordnance office phoned Jacobson to ask if he could make 5,240,000 shot-shell cartridges by the end of the year. These were for aircraft emergency kits, usable in the Colt .45 automatic pistol. A flier downed at sea or in the jungle could kill fish or small game at short ranges with the 135 little lead pellets packed in each shell, a miniature shotgun charge. Without previous knowledge or experience with this novelty, Evansville completed the order on time. To do so, it worked Sundays and Christmas day.

A little more than a year later, the local papers carried a letter from Milton D. Rothschild, who had been basement manager of an Evansville department store on December 7, 1941, and now was a sergeant of the Air Force in the Burma-China theater.

"I have just got back from Assam after spending eight days walking out of the Hump," he wrote. "I am a radio operator and flying the Hump into China regularly. The pilot, co-pilot and I were forced to bail out and, on landing, I found myself isolated. I opened my jungle kit and there, right on top, was a package

of shells made in my home town. It sorta made me feel good out there in the middle of nowhere to see the Chrysler Evansville Arsenal's name. I wanted to write and thank you all, as the shot came in very handy."

A little later Ordnance gave the arsenal an order for 3,000,000 rounds of blanks and 2,000,000 rounds of dummy .45 cartridges. The blanks are used in the training of war dogs; fired over the dog's head until it no longer flinches, then into its face until the dog is satisfied that a pistol and its noise are harmless to him. The dummies are used for the functional testing of loading and ejecting.

Employment had reached a peak of 12,655 in September, 1943. It was down to 7,951 by early January, reached a low of 2,401 May 31, 1944. These two thousand stayed on for the repacking of a billion and a half rounds of .45 and .30 ammunition between then and October.

BULLETS SEALED IN CANS

These cartridges had been packed originally by Chrysler and other makers in containers of double-dipped, heavy, waxed paper enclosed in heavy wooden boxes. Ample protection in the past and in the fighting in Africa and Italy, the pack failed to stand up in the South Pacific and by midsummer of 1943 General MacArthur was asking for a better one. Ordnance gave Evansville an engineering project to develop such a pack, out of which grew a heavy gauge

Early in the war shipping boxes contained 1800 cartridges.
Here an inspector is checking part of one day's shipment.

can made by the American Can Co., hermetically
sealed, opened with a turn key like a can of corned
beef, and capable of being resealed with scotch tape if
all the contents should not be used at first opening.

The hermetic sealing of the can was all-important
in the tropics and in amphibious warfare and no satisfactory testing apparatus existed on the market. The
arsenal first improvised an ordinary glass bell jar with
a vacuum which, in theory, would draw bubbles from
a leaking can.

Bob Dickman, assistant Plant Engineer, was given
the task of finding a better way and, almost over-

night, designed the "Vacuveyor," since patented and made standard in all small arms plants by Ordnance directive. Postwar, it is expected to be widely used by food canners and the like. The original machine was put together at Evansville of heavy steel plates, 45 feet long, 13 feet high and 5 feet wide, this tank filled with water under vacuum pressure. An electric conveyor carried 700 ammunition cans hourly through the tank, inspectors watching through heavy plastic windows. An imperfect can disclosed itself by tell-tale bubbles and was discarded as it emerged. More than two million cans and a million reinforced wooden boxes were used in the repack.

Ordnance soon extended the use of the can to all

Chrysler made 485,448,758 of these .30 caliber carbine cartridges.

small calibers, even to 20 mm. artillery shells. General Kirk in May, 1945, told Mr. Jacobson that the repackaging program was the greatest single contribution made to the war by the Evansville arsenal, exceeding even its successful production of steel cases.

This final ammunition contract had to be carried out coincidentally with the dispersal of $23,000,000 of production machinery, including nearly 4,000 machine tools. Crews worked night and day to clear 400,000 square feet for the new tank job, leaving 150,000 square feet open for the repacking. Two hundred and forty-two railroad cars of machinery were shipped to storage at the Vigo, Indiana, arsenal, 114 more car lots to storage at Lake City, Missouri.

Inspecting the .30 caliber steel cartridge case after coming from its anti-corrosion bath.

Evansville's closing down left Ordnance without a source of steel cups for the .45. This job was given to Frankford Arsenal and Evansville shipped such presses and die blocks as Frankford wanted. Cup production in steel being strange to them, they asked Evansville's aid, and Earl Parker, foreman of blanking and cupping, was sent to Philadelphia on loan.

"The blanking and cupping of .45 steel cups now is under way here," Frankford wrote Jacobson in August, 1944. "The successful performance of these operations is largely due to the expert advice and direction of your Mr. Earl Parker during the past five days. His competence and very willing cooperation reflect credit upon himself and the Chrysler Corporation. It is typical of the team work which has characterized relations between Frankford Arsenal and your company."

The more units a factory produces, the more costly an undetected mistake. Turning out as many as 12,500,000 cartridges in a day, an overlooked error at Evansville could compound itself by the millions within one shift.

THE EVANSVILLE BELT LINE

This was one justification for the nearly six miles of motorized belt and gravity roller conveyors installed, possibly never equaled in a plant of comparable size. It insured the smooth, unbroken flow of

Chrysler made blank cartridges for the training of K-9 war dogs. Blanks taught the dogs not to fear the sight or sound of guns.

production from machine to inspection, and the discovery within a few ticks of the clock of something gone wrong.

One conveyor line alone was two and a half miles long, this endless belt carrying the unloaded cartridges from the factory across country to the explosives area and bringing the loaded cartridges back. It did the work of twenty-eight 2½-ton trucks, one loaded every three minutes. Such a flow of trucks would have demanded its own highway and traffic police. The belt lines did the hauling automatically, safely and almost imperceptibly. Though they cost $920,-000, they paid for themselves within three months over the cost of manual handling.

More than a billion and a half cartridges were repacked at Evansville in heavy-gauge, air-tight cans for MacArthur.

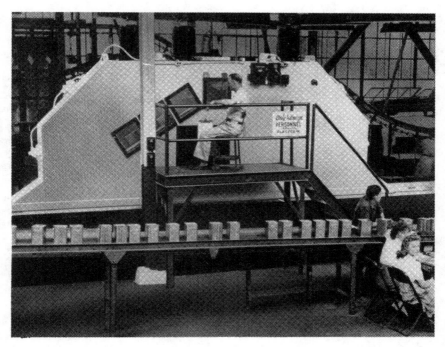

The solution of the air-tight pack—the Vacuveyor, invented almost overnight by Plant Engineer Dickman and patented in his name.

The hand feeding of the cartridge gauging machines called for 314 women. The introduction of unscramblers and of feeder conveyors to the water-proofing and gauging machines eliminated 208 of these operators at a yearly saving to the Government of $913,735. Plant Engineering claimed a similar saving of nearly a million dollars yearly for machine packing over hand of the finished cartridge.

An $8,500 conveyor and elevator installation in bullet assembly saved an estimated $115,000 a year. The bullets had been carried and dumped by hand into the rumblers, toted by hand again from the

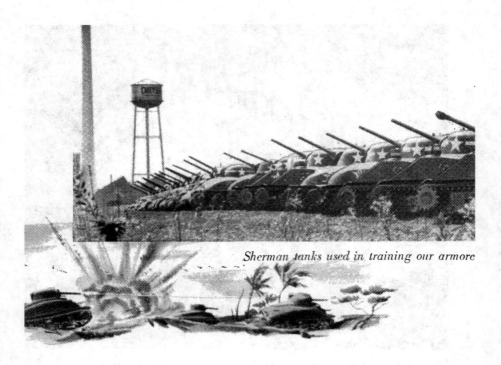

Sherman tanks used in training our armore

rumblers, first to Chrysler inspectors, then to Ordnance inspection. A similar installation in case inspection brought an equivalent saving.

Explosives were the farthest removed from Chrysler's normal work. This and their own fascination made them the most interesting part of the job to the men and women who filled this war contract.

Any hour there were enough highly explosive detonators and initiators in the explosives area to blow a deep hole in the Ohio valley, with no help from the propellant powders. Men who would have winced at a shotgun discharge, women who would have stopped their ears at the sight of a pistol in a play, handled these materials eight hours a day.

54

es were returned to Evansville to be completely rebuilt before seeing action.

The carbine primer was a mixture of three chemicals which can not be named, a high explosive combination. Engineering did more research, probably, on the primer than on all the rest of the cartridge combined. Ralph Jones and his men were made frantic by their inconstancy; the same batch would test differently from hour to hour. Jones appealed to Engineering which set up a small group to study detonators and nothing else.

After failing to find any appreciable variation in the prime ingredients, this group discovered that what happened to the stuff after mixing held the answers. The variations arose from six causes: temperature and humidity where stored, where inspected and where tested; minute differences in pellet weights; effects arising from inserting the primers into cases for testing; and the length of time during which they were exposed to an uncontrolled atmosphere.

The tear-down line. When the tank was dismantled, every detail was cleaned and either replaced or made good as new.

There was no further difficulty after the charging rooms had been air-conditioned. The reader may ask why the whole explosives area was not air-conditioned to begin with, the benefits being so obvious. Cost and scarcity is the answer; it would have cost several hundred thousands of dollars, if the equipment could have been had in the midst of war.

How greatly safety is a matter of organized caution was dramatized at Evansville. Over two years during which 3,250,000 pounds of powder and 275,000 pounds of high explosives were handled, there was no serious accident and many fewer minor ones than in the average factory where there are no abnormal hazards. In fact, the explosives industry had in 1944 the second best accident record in America, excelled only by the women's garment trade.

EVERY SAFETY PRECAUTION TAKEN

The principle of handling high explosives safely is never to fear but always to respect their power, and to keep reducing the quantities. Fear makes for nervousness and nervousness may be as productive of accidents as is carelessness. The most dangerous compound used at Evansville was the .30 caliber carbine primer. It was made 12 pounds at a time in an automatic, remotely-controlled machine which was no more than a baker's dough mixer. Twelve pounds was enough for 180,000 primers—only 1/25th of a grain went into each cup.

Only one-ninth of this quantity or a little more than a pound was handled, in its wet state, at one time by the men who loaded the primer cups. This quantity was cut in half again when the primers went to the dry house where the moisture was baked out. Now much more dangerous in their dried-out state, the unit was reduced to 2,000 cups or about a quarter of a pound when the primers were canned for storage. Finally, when they went to the primer inverting machines to be pressed into the heads of cartridges no more than 700 were handled at a time. That is, the quantity steadily was reduced as the danger increased.

All buildings were spaced according to the time-tested quantity-distance tables of Ordnance. The walls were thick, the roofs flimsy; in case of a touch-off, the force would shoot upward. Where the danger was the greatest, heavy concrete or earthwork deflectors flanked the storage warehouses in order that the detonation of one might not set off the others.

Temperature and humidity were watched closely. Where refrigeration was necessary, ice was used, not so much for fear of an electric box arcing as for the moisture office. The high humidity of the Ohio valley is ideal for the handling of explosives. In summer relative humidity often registers 80-86 day after day,

higher than the controlled atmosphere of the charging rooms.

Most explosives can be handled with impunity if wet enough. The .30 primer mix looked like granulated mud as the chargers rolled and worked it into series of little holes in a steel plate looking something

like a cribbage board. The much less flighty .45 primer mixture, paradoxically, gave more trouble. The reason was that 19% of moisture content is permissible in the .30 primer on the charging tables. The specifications call for the .45 primer to be worked at 10% of moisture; at 8% it will spark, and there were a number of

Army trucks used by our troops in training went through the same reconditioning given tanks at Evansville.

59

flashes from it, none serious. It burns, fortunately, when not confined, where the .30 primer mix detonates.

Good housekeeping was another prime safety caution. One hour in eight on the charging beds and foiling presses was given to cleaning and scrubbing. At every change of shift and stop for lunch, there was a general housecleaning. The .30 primer waste was collected from the machine sumps in small cotton bags which, saturated, went into a special furnace at 1400 degrees, insuring instant combustion.

Lightning is an uncontrollable hazard, high in the Ohio valley, yet one which can be guarded against. Twenty-five special weather stations were set up by the Department of Commerce to the South, West

and North of Evansville to warn of approaching
thunder storms—electrical storms from the East are
unknown there. Without this information every dark
cloud would have posed a problem of whether or not
to shut down.

Three men from Safety trained in elementary
meteorology at the Department of Commerce school
in Chicago were made responsible for charting storms
and ordering the area evacuated if need be. On their
warning, the mixing houses were closed at once, but
as a minimum notice of fifteen minutes was given, the
loading areas cleaned up all primers before stopping
work, dried-out primers being nearly as dangerous as
lightning.

Primer mixtures were trundled from the mixing
houses to the loading buildings or to storage in a kind
of low-slung baby-buggy, sometimes known as an

angel-buggy. The bodies were wood, the frames of non-sparking metals, the tires rubber. Equipped with a "dead man's brake," the carts could not move until pushed, and their center of gravity was so low they could not be overturned by accident.

The mixture was distributed in rubber cups. The buggy-pusher did not enter the loading buildings, leaving the cups in a compartment having both an inner and outer door like the kitchen milk chute common in many American cities, and cooled and kept moist with ice. All employees in the danger areas were supplied with conductive shoes which automatically dissipated bodily electrical charges into copper wiring embedded in the cement floors, before these charges could accumulate to the sparking point. Matches and lighters were strictly taboo, though smoking was permitted in the lunch rooms at meal periods. Smokers were required, however, to use lighters attached to the walls.

The introduction of the double-based carbine cartridge containing nitroglycerine upset all the quantity-distance safety tables upon which the area had been laid out, forcing Ordnance to buy 400 acres some nine miles north of the arsenal as a powder farm. A series of widely-spaced concrete igloos flanked by fortress-like deflectors was completed in October, 1943.

Ralph Jones had no man of previous experience with explosives, did not want one. "We couldn't have hoped to get good ones in the midst of war," he ex-

Thousands of the newest type firebombs—the M-74—were also made in the Evansville Plant.

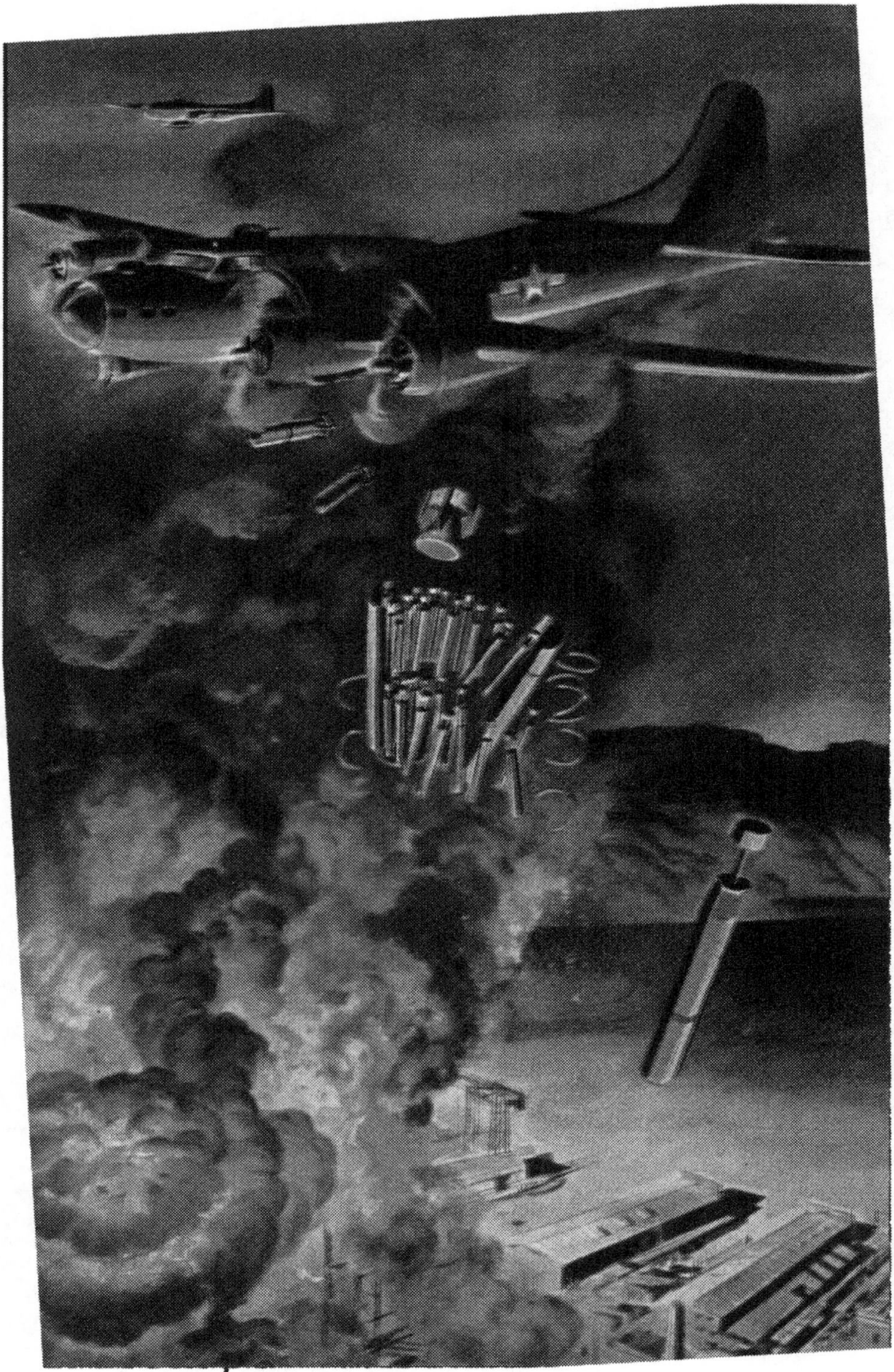

Evansville was commissioned to make 7,500,000 of the small bombs shown on the right. These were delivered in clusters of 38 put together into 500-pound bombs as shown on the left.

plained, "while a little knowledge is worse than none in this business." For primer-chargers, he asked Employment to find him tall, lean men, on the theory that they are alert and cat-like. For angel-buggy chauffeurs, he asked for older men, the fat preferred. "Slow and easy did it there," he said.

PUBLIC WAS INVITED TO VISIT PLANT

Work in an ammunition plant sounds dangerous to the average man or woman and, given a choice, few will choose it. Evansville was awhisper with scare stories about the arsenal in the early days of the project. It was, so the rumors went, a daring thing to ride by in a car; to work there would be the direst folly. Once a working force was hired, it easily could be educated out of this state of mind, but if these stories should be widely believed it would not be easy to find workers in the thousands.

Instead of trying to attack a baseless fear directly, management went to work on the sources of public opinion. Various influential groups were conducted through the plant while it was in operation. These tours were so thorough that they were broken up by luncheon served in the arsenal. When the visitors themselves had been satisfied that cartridge-loading is no more dangerous than work in a shipyard, an aircraft plant or a chain grocery, they were asked to do their part in quelling wild talk. Their national and local patriotism was invoked. The local ministers

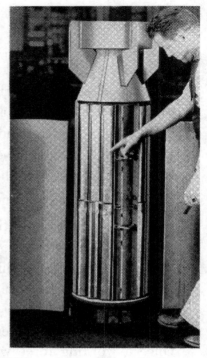

Showing how the small ten-pound incendiaries are loaded into large clusters.

were followed by the school teachers, then by the doctors and other groups.

It worked and quickly. The visit of the doctors had another useful result. Too many employees had been turning in physicians' certificates that they were unable to work, though their health seemed as robust as any's. When the Army's and Navy's great need of ammunition had been dramatized to the doctors and they had seen for themselves that there were no unusual health hazards in the work, the flow of sick certificates became a trickle and the absentee problem dwindled to a minor one, while the widespread public familiarity with the arsenal created a community good will no less useful to any business in war than in peace.

A MILLION ROUNDS TEST-FIRED MONTHLY

The chatter of machine guns and the bark of carbines, pistols and revolvers was nearly continuous on the twenty-six firing ranges of the Ballistics building. Test-firing is another form of inspection, another way

66

of preventing production mistakes from laying a million eggs before discovery. There can be no greater tragedy in war than for a soldier's gun to fail him when he needs it, and Ordnance takes extreme precautions to avoid this. The only certain way to find out whether a cartridge is good being to fire it, Chrysler's men and women gunners fired 850,000 rounds a month. Ordnance gunners at the arsenal another 200,000 rounds.

At the start of each shift twenty bullets were taken from each bullet machine. To remove the possibility of variations in the test-firing being caused by variations in the loading machines, all were loaded in the same dial loader and fired ten rounds to a target. Each bullet was identified to the bullet machine which had formed it. The targets came back to girl tabulators who quickly charted any deviation. A target out of line led either to the resampling of the suspect machine or to shutting it down for correction. Experience demonstrated that a bullet machine or loader started right would stay right through a shift.

Though all powder is tested repeatedly at the mills which make it, it was tested again on receipt at Evansville and a quantity from each shipment stored for a week in a cabinet under a constant temperature of 120 degrees and relative humidity of 75-85. At the end of the week this was tested against untreated powder from the same shipment and the divergence had to fall within set limits. As a test of uniformity, samples were taken from six packages and blended, then fired comparatively with cartridges loaded from each of the six packages.

Ballistics tested the powder once more before it was loaded, but as established velocity may not remain constant in production for a day or a week, a number of finished rounds were collected from each of the 180 dial loaders at the start of each shift and tried for pressure, accuracy, function and casualty.

Between seven and eight thousand rounds were fired daily from fixed gun mounts with heavy 20-inch barrels for velocity, pressure and accuracy testing. Such guns being already aimed and the gunner having only to pull the trigger, most of this firing was done by girls. Men fired the sub-machine guns, carbines, pistols and revolvers, men who loved guns and marvelled that anybody could be found to pay them for shooting.

As the .45 caliber cartridge is used in many weapons, Ballistics test-fired it in all—three different models of the Thompson sub-machine gun, the "Chicago typewriter" of gang warfare; the Reising sub-machine gun used by the Marine Corps; the new and exciting M-3 sub-machine gun; the Colt .45 automatic pistol and the Colt and the Smith & Wesson .45 revolvers. The revolvers have not been made for years and only 80,000 remain in Ordnance stores.

INCENDIARY BOMB (PTI), M74

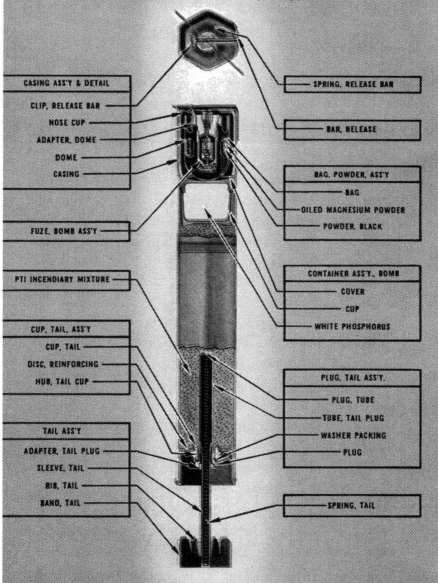

CASING ASS'Y & DETAIL
CLIP, RELEASE BAR
NOSE CUP
ADAPTER, DOME
DOME
CASING

FUZE, BOMB ASS'Y

PTI INCENDIARY MIXTURE

CUP, TAIL, ASS'Y
CUP, TAIL
DISC, REINFORCING
HUB, TAIL CUP

TAIL ASS'Y
ADAPTER, TAIL PLUG
SLEEVE, TAIL
RIB, TAIL
BAND, TAIL

SPRING, RELEASE BAR

BAR, RELEASE

BAG, POWDER, ASS'Y
BAG
OILED MAGNESIUM POWDER
POWDER, BLACK

CONTAINER ASS'Y., BOMB
COVER
CUP
WHITE PHOSPHORUS

PLUG, TAIL ASS'Y.
PLUG, TUBE
TUBE, TAIL PLUG
WASHER PACKING
PLUG

SPRING, TAIL

The revolvers long ago were driven out by the famous Colt automatic, .45 pistol of 1911, developed to stop the Moro when he ran amok. Until then, the American soldier carried a .38 revolver. The writer once saw a Moro run amok in the street of Mindanao village, armed with a kris. An officer of the Philippine Scouts began firing with his .38 when the maddened native was 30 feet away. Though all six shots hit their mark, only the last stopped the Moro when he was not more than six feet from the gun.

The Army asked for a weapon which would turn a man over on his back if the slug hit him above the knees, flop him on his face if it struck below the knees. Though marked for replacement by the new carbine, the Army still loves and asks for its .45 automatic.

The new M-3, lightest of all machine guns, is made of stampings except for three parts, and has a barrel which can be made much faster than conventional barrels and so can be turned out in huge volume at low cost. This rugged, all-metal weapon suggesting

What happened when the firebomb touched the earth; test firing one by night at Evansville.

something out of Buck Rogers first came off a production line on April 30, 1943. So smartly was procurement set up that the gun was only ten months from the first sketch on the drawing board to mass production.

THE SWASTIKA ON THE PHONE BOOK

No plant is more vulnerable to sabotage than one which makes ammunition, yet in two years the only scare turned up by Plant Protection was the finding of a swastika drawn on the cover of a plant telephone book. The swastika turned out to be an idle doodle quickly traced to a recent graduate in journalism at the University of Indiana and former cub reporter on a Washington, D.C., newspaper, who also was by way of being an amateur cartoonist. He readily admitted the design, saying he had thought nothing of it then, thought less of it now. Plant Protection gave him a clean bill of health after checking his history.

71

Evansville, with a population of 97,000 in 1940, could not of itself supply the army of workers needed by its war industries, though thousands of housewives and school girls became wage earners for the first time. Nor could the city, even with Government emergency housing, begin to house the influx of outside labor. This led to an extraordinary labor condition. At the peak of employment at the Chrysler arsenal, 2,591 men and women or 21% of the payroll were travelling more than 25 miles a day each way to and from work, most of them in private automobiles.

Vincennes, Indiana, 52 miles from Evansville, sent 113 to work at Chrysler. Owensboro, Kentucky, 41 miles up river, sent 365. Sixty-five Chrysler workers came and went daily from Madisonville, Kentucky, 60 miles distant, 19 from Harrisburg, Illinois, 75 miles away. Conditions at the shipyard, Republic, Servel, Sunbeam, Briggs and Hoosier Lamp were similar. As tires and gas became harder and harder to get, the problem grew to be critical and was solved only by the cut in small arms schedules late in 1943.

The arsenal won its Army-Navy "E" flag in the early summer of 1943. Making the award, Lt. Col. Miles Chatfield of Philadelphia said: "Ninety days after you broke ground, you proof-fired the first ammunition made at this plant. When the Chief of Ordnance asked you to switch from brass to steel you did the seemingly impossible and then when you were

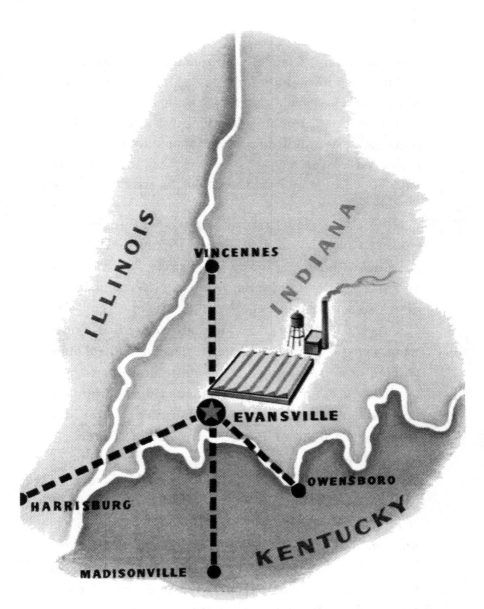

More than one-fifth of the arsenal employees travelled more than 50 miles a day to and from their jobs, usually by car.

asked to convert some of your machines to .30 caliber carbine ammunition, you made the first cup within a week and two weeks later you proof-fired the first round of that ammunition. This all adds up to a remarkable accomplishment performed by those inexperienced in the ways of making ammunition, but with a willingness and devotion to patriotic duty second to none."

H. E. Clive of the British Ministry of Supply Purchasing Commission visited the arsenal in 1943. In writing Mr. Jacobson "how very grateful we are toward you and your company for your very open and frank discussions on your wonderful achievement," Mr. Clive went on to say: "You undoubtedly have shown what can be achieved by such careful control and studied organization in the manufacture of this particular type of ammunition. So far as the manufacture of small arms ammunition is concerned, I consider yours is the outstanding achievement of this war."

This is a letter from Capt. George R. McMullen of the Philadelphia Ordnance office to Mr. Jacobson: "For some weeks, the writer has had the privilege of reading Bob Christman's weekly engineering reports and, in my judgment, they have been consistently outstanding documents week after week. With so much paper work and reports floating around these days, it is a pleasure to read something that is brief, concise, intelligent and to the point."

74

Evansville proudly flew its "E" flag
along with the Stars and Stripes.

When ammunition production ended, General Kirk, chief of the Small Arms section, wrote Mr. Jacobson: "The Evansville plant did a remarkable job in supplying the Government with vast quantities of ammunition and it is with regret that we found it necessary to relinquish its facilities, making it available for other war work. We in the Ordnance department, and particularly in the Small Arms division, appreciate deeply the work performed at Evansville and the cooperation we have had from every one associated with the ammunition program at your plant."

Early in 1944, Rep. Albert J. Engel made a House-authorized investigation of the production records and costs of Army Ordnance ammunition plants. His report to the House on June 21, 1944, praised Ordnance and its contractors highly. In sending a copy of this report to Mr. Keller, Maj. Gen. L. H. Campbell Jr., Chief of Ordnance, wrote: "You and all your associates who have had such a large part in this achievement richly deserve the thanks of all of us for your help. The Under Secretary of War, Mr. Robert

P. Patterson, and the Chief of the Army Service Forces, Lt. Gen. Brehon Somervell, have characterized Representative Engel's report as a well-deserved tribute. To their congratulations, I add my own. We of Ordnance are proud of this record which reflects splendidly the cooperative relationship long existing between American industry and Army Ordnance."

The End

CPSIA information can be obtained
at www.ICGtesting.com
Printed in the USA
LVHW081645200122
709000LV00014B/1340